Δ The Triangle Papers: 36

EAST-WEST RELATIONS

A Task Force Report to
The Trilateral Commission

Authors: VALÉRY GISCARD D'ESTAING
Member of the National Assembly and Chairman of the
Foreign Affairs Committee; former President of the
French Republic

YASUHIRO NAKASONE
Member of the Diet; former Prime Minister of Japan

HENRY A. KISSINGER
Chairman, Kissinger Associates, Inc.; former U.S.
Secretary of State; former U.S. Assistant to the President
for National Security Affairs

© Copyright, 1989. The Trilateral Commission
All Rights Reserved.

Library of Congress Cataloging-in-Publication Data

Giscard d'Estaing, Valéry, 1926-
  East-West Relations.

  (The Triangle Papers ; 36)
    1. World politics—1985-1995. 2. Soviet Union—Foreign relations—
  1985- .   I. Nakasone, Yasuhiro, 1918- .   II. Kissinger, Henry, 1923- .
  III. Title.   IV. Series.

D849.G54 1989   327'.09'048   89-4989
ISBN 0-930503-06-6

Manufactured in the United States of America

THE TRILATERAL COMMISSION

345 East 46th Street   c/o Japan Center for   35, avenue de Friedland
New York, NY 10017   International Exchange   75008 Paris, France
                                    4-9-17 Minami-Azabu
                                        Minato-ku
                                       Tokyo, Japan

Table of Contents

Authors' Foreword

East-West relations have entered a new phase. Changes in the Soviet Union's domestic and foreign policies have already affected the climate of East-West relations and, in some areas, its substance. Mikhail Gorbachev's new policies suggest new approaches to the future of the Soviet Union's domestic system, its foreign policies, and East-West relations. It would be a mistake, however, to analyze these developments or to devise Western policies in terms of a single personality; to be lasting they must take into account the fundamental necessities facing the Soviet Union and the opportunities before the democracies.

We have prepared this report in the belief that our countries face a challenge that will shape the future of international relations for several decades. So far, our countries have not reached a consensus on the significance of this challenge, on the degree to which it reflects a lasting change in Soviet policies, or even on our own attitudes in relation to it.

Some believe that, until much more has changed in the Soviet Union, the industrial democracies should wait prudently on the sidelines or continue the same general policies they have pursued since World War II. Others argue that the Soviet threat has changed so completely that the existing defense and political arrangements can be dramatically altered.

Based on our collective experience of dealing with the Communist world, discussions with present Soviet leaders including Mr. Gorbachev, and studies by experts in the West, we believe that our countries have a rare opportunity to change the nature of East-West relations in ways beneficial to the West, provided they develop a clear agenda and strategy. On the other hand, passivity or—worse—a posture of delayed and uncoordinated reaction to Soviet initiatives would enable the Kremlin to define the East-West agenda and serve primarily Soviet interests.

Few would contest that our countries have a profound stake in developments inside the Soviet Union. For more than four decades, protecting our national security and the freedom of other peoples from Soviet expansionism has placed a tremendous burden on our countries and occasionally on our relationships with each other. During this period we have had to live with the threat of devastating conflict. We take pride in the fact that defenses have been maintained and military conflict deterred.

We do not expect to reduce these burdens substantially overnight. Mr. Gorbachev cannot wish away the fundamental differences in systems, outlooks and interests that have separated the Soviet bloc from the non-Communist world. Nor should our leaders expect this. Change will come slowly and ambivalently. In the meantime, our countries will have to remain strong and vigilant. A successful transformation to a more peaceful East-West relationship is not guaranteed. New foundations for East-West relations, if they are to be solid, must be built arduously—brick by brick.

SOVIET TRENDS

General

Our assessment of the Soviet Union is based on two premises. First, the pressures for change in Soviet domestic and foreign policies reflect a crisis of the Communist system and not simply the personal preferences of a particular Soviet leader; second, the relaxation of East-West tensions in the late 1980s is qualitatively different from earlier periods of détente.

In Mikhail Gorbachev the Soviet Union has found an exceptional leader, quite unlike any of his predecessors. In his personal style and flair, Mr. Gorbachev has embraced reform more quickly and comprehensively than another leader might have done. We are persuaded, however, that it is the objective necessities confronting the Soviet Union which establish both the need for change as well as its direction. Were Mr. Gorbachev to leave the scene, these realities would probably sustain his general course and direction, albeit at a slower pace and with a less ebullient style.

For any Soviet leader would have had to try to revitalize the economy and overcome the persistent social malaise. Similarly, the deployment—contrary to Soviet expectations—of U.S. intermediate nuclear forces in Western Europe in response to the Soviet military build-up, the extended crisis in Poland, the long dispute with China, the chilly relationship with Japan, and the failure of Soviet military intervention in Afghanistan—have combined to impose a reappraisal of Soviet foreign policy.

Our countries need to define a strategy based on a correct assessment of the necessities propelling the Soviet Union toward sweeping domestic reform and reduced confrontation with the West. We believe that these changes are likely to occur more quickly under Mr. Gorbachev's continued leadership than they would were his known political rivals in charge.

At the same time, quite different equilibria between economic and political reforms could occur. Conceivably, accelerated efforts to meet popular aspirations for improvement in the standard of living could be balanced by a reinforcement of central political authority, on the Chinese pattern.

The new Soviet diplomacy has an unprecedented sweep. It addresses not only the standard military issues, but political and regional concerns. In addition to arms control issues, the Soviets have sought accommodations in some regional conflicts, notably Afghanistan. The combination, if implemented, amounts to a new concept of security. The West can do no less than develop its own coherent policy and security agenda.

Mr. Gorbachev has stated in public, and has reaffirmed to us, his belief that if it is to carry out its domestic reform program, the Soviet Union needs to improve its relations with the outside world. The high priority given to domestic reform in the Soviet agenda is, in fact, of greater significance for our countries than whether or not these reforms actually succeed. For the priority of domestic reform, if nothing else, deflects energies from the traditional Cold War agenda.

The importance of the reform program derives in part from the crisis of confidence that is so evident in the Soviet Union today. Past Soviet leaders had little doubt about the ultimate superiority of the socialist economic system; despite the large gap between Soviet and Western living standards, they believed that it was only a matter of time before Communism caught up to and surpassed the advanced capitalist countries. The collapse of this hope—reinforced by the daily comparisons afforded by instantaneous global communications—rendered unavoidable the change of course introduced by Mr. Gorbachev. Even two years ago, when perestroika (restructuring) was just starting, there was great expectation that the economy would quickly respond to the reforms envisaged by Mr. Gorbachev. As it turned out, the difficulties of implementing the reform program, its complexity, and the long lag between reforms and concrete results were greatly underestimated.

The Soviet Union we saw in January of this year was much more somber. The optimism of past years has vanished; we found a new, more realistic awareness of the enormous difficulties the Soviets face merely to achieve growth, much less to begin to close the gap with the capitalist democracies. This backdrop of pervasive pessimism impels Mr. Gorbachev to reinvigorate the Soviet economy by accelerating restructuring. This dilemma rather than some abstract pacifist philosophy is driving the Soviet leader to reduce tensions in international relations. He has every incentive to reduce the share of military spending in Soviet GNP and to seek beneficial economic relationships, including foreign investment, with the non-socialist countries.

Domestic Reforms
After four years in power, Mr. Gorbachev's economic program has in our view created a great deal of turmoil without achieving much in

substance. Even relatively minor reforms have evoked a backlash; for instance, the freedom to form cooperatives has been opposed by conservatives and significant parts of public opinion on the ground that they foster unjustifiable inequality and excessive privilege. And the offer of long-term agricultural leases to private farmers has not generated an adequate number of candidates willing to accept the offer, because of a preference of many for the safer, more familiar and less demanding position of a salaried employee on a collective farm or simply because of the fear that this policy could be reversed. And the more fundamental and wrenching reforms of price structure and convertibility of the ruble have not even been attempted. Although Mr. Gorbachev overcame a conservative reaction last year, many of the reforms are still opposed by large segments of the Soviet administration, and at the top the struggle over the direction of future Soviet policies continues. In the meantime, the nationalities problem has become acute, notably in the Baltic states, in Armenia, and in Georgia.

Thus, the Soviet leader faces several dilemmas. Economic reforms require decentralization of power. Yet, at the beginning, decentralization creates new confusion and reduces the leadership's ability to control the direction of change. More crucially, decentralization challenges the very legitimacy of the Soviet style of socialism based on highly centralized authority. Glasnost is intended to win popular support for the reforms, but at the same time provides the intelligentsia with an opportunity to criticize the slow pace of perestroika and to dispute specific aspects of the reform program. Thus, perestroika is under attack from conservatives, for whom it goes too far, and from intellectuals, for whom it does not go far enough.

The recent elections in the Soviet Union illustrate this ambivalence. The results were helpful to Gorbachev by weakening a number of conservative opponents to his reforms. At the same time they demonstrated a restiveness with the slow pace of economic progress, that weakens the Communist Party, and turns the demands for accelerated economic improvement into the dominant feature of Soviet political life. Dissatisfaction with perestroika is therefore likely to take the form of demands for more dramatic economic changes rather than for a return to traditional Communist patterns.

Finally, the reforms can only show results for the average Soviet citizen in the long term, while entrenched interests are hurt immediately by necessary adjustments. As in China, price reform is a prerequisite for the success of the reform program but, in the near term, is politically explosive. The mounting threat of inflation will add supplementary arguments to postpone the reforms.

These dilemmas make the implementation of Gorbachev's reform program difficult and risky. At the same time, the Soviet Union's stake in it is enormous since it is fundamentally an effort to sustain superpower status into the 21st century and to achieve a level of economic development at least not too distant from those of the United States, the European Community, and Japan. It is now obvious that the road to success will be long and very difficult. The absolute prerequisite is a radical transformation of the Soviet system that will bring the USSR closer to Western concepts of market economics and democratic institutions. *That is the definition of perestroika which the present authors support.*

Foreign Policy
The domestic reform program generates the "new thinking" in Soviet foreign policy in two important if somewhat contradictory ways.

- On the one hand, in conversation with us and in his public speeches, Mr. Gorbachev explicitly links the need for "predictability" in foreign relations to the Soviet Union's need to concentrate on the domestic agenda: "Our foreign policy is today, to a greater extent than ever before, determined by domestic policy, by our interest in concentrating our efforts on constructive activities aimed at improving our country. And that is why we need a lasting peace, predictability and constructive new international relations."

- On the other hand, because Mr. Gorbachev's domestic freedom of maneuver is limited and highly susceptible to failure, he tends increasingly to look for successes in foreign policy as compensation. This tempts him to weaken, if not break, the links between the United States and its allies in Western Europe and Asia, and in general to push the United States back to the Western Hemisphere. This strategy must be resisted by the democratic countries.

In pursuit of the first strand of this policy—that of genuine accommodation—Mr. Gorbachev's new approach has challenged some of the fundamental precepts of traditional Soviet and even of imperial Russian foreign policy. He has stated that Soviet security cannot be achieved at the price of the insecurity of other countries. The value of a massive build-up of strategic weapons as a political strategy has been challenged in debates within the Soviet Union. The traditional reliance on a huge number of troops and massive conventional superiority is being questioned even in senior military circles. This change of attitude is evident in the Soviet withdrawal from Afghanistan and the pressure placed on Vietnam to withdraw its forces from Cambodia. It is unprecedented that the Soviet Union should have accepted the risk of the collapse of a Communist government in Afghanistan.

The decision to reduce Soviet troop strength by 500,000, which Gorbachev announced before the UN General Assembly in December 1988, is probably designed to reduce the enormous budget deficit and above all to modernize the swollen Soviet armed forces. Nevertheless, it should be welcomed as a first step towards reciprocal and equitable reduction of conventional forces.

In pursuit of the second strand of Soviet policy, there are still major areas where Soviet policies are challenging the United States and its allies. For example, in our discussions with Soviet leaders, it was clear that the Soviet Union is not yet willing to implement in Eastern Europe the principle of non-intervention that Mr. Gorbachev proclaimed before the United Nations and that of equal relationships which he seems to be practicing with respect to China. The Soviet Union has also proved unwilling to recognize Japan's claim to the "Northern Territories" occupied by the USSR. It continues to support regimes hostile to the United States in the Western Hemisphere.

The USSR will remain a major military power in Eurasia. So long as its relative military advantages persist, the threat of force will remain a significant factor in international relations. The democracies have a common interest in resisting the strategy of pushing the United States back to the Western Hemisphere. For were it to prove successful, the Soviet Union could then use its central geographic position to weaken and divide its neighbors one by one. Certain aspects of current Soviet policy, especially in Europe, are consistent with this long-term objective.

Thus, the democracies must learn to deal with Gorbachev's style, which is to flood the Western decision-making process with a rapid series of unilateral moves, some of them involving genuine concessions, others relying largely on psychological warfare. If real progress is to be made, Western policy must winnow the real concessions from the propagandistic overtures, and respond on two levels: to the substance, and to the public relations aspect. We must develop our own initiatives and policies and put forth our own ideas that reflect what our countries understand by a peaceful world and that reflect the aspirations of our people for progress and democracy.

THE TRILATERAL AGENDA

The Strategic Relationship

A new strategic dialogue between East and West is taking shape. It has been given impetus by the signing of the INF treaty, the convocation of negotiations on conventional weapons and forces in Vienna, and the progress made between the United States and the Soviet Union in the negotiations on the reduction of strategic weapons.

A common theme in this new dialogue is the desirability of achieving substantial reductions in some categories of weapons and forces. Mr. Gorbachev has adopted this theme; it was his ostensible rationale for agreeing to the zero option in the INF talks. He has also proposed the elimination of short-range nuclear weapons in Europe; at Vienna his delegation has proposed a three-stage reduction of conventional forces and major weapons systems to levels well below NATO's current posture; and he has announced a unilateral reduction of 500,000 in armed forces, including the withdrawal of tanks and tank divisions from Eastern Europe as well as the reduction of forces in East Asia.

We also note that various Soviet spokesmen, echoing Gorbachev, speak of adopting "defensive" defense and the criterion of "reasonable sufficiency" to measure their forces—suggesting the possibility of a major shift in Soviet military doctrine. All of this remains to be tested in negotiations and in the actual disposition of forces as well as military practice, rather than by wishful thinking.

Such initiatives strike a responsive chord in Western public opinion and contribute to pressures to reduce defense expenditures. They generate a debate about which categories should be given priority in reductions—tactical nuclear or conventional—and how far the West can go in reducing its nuclear forces without weakening its defense and deterrent capacity. In the background there is the older debate about the role of arms control in safeguarding security, and the linkage between arms control and geopolitical issues. There is in addition an unfortunate tendency to treat defense and arms control as alternatives rather than as complementary issues.

Our analysis of the strategic situation is based on three premises:

(1) The pressure for reductions in the Soviet Union reflects in part economic necessity, that is to say, the impossibility of meeting the economic goals of perestroika under conditions of an arms race. This is all the more true because until now the democracies have proved resilient enough to maintain a rough military balance at whatever level was required.

(2) In part Soviet moves may reflect a strategic design: the Soviet leaders may believe that the central geographic location of the Soviet Union and its superiority in conventional forces and mobilizable reserves confer on it an inherent advantage in any program of arms reductions.

(3) Nevertheless, the democracies should welcome making arms reduction a central theme of the East-West dialogue *provided* they keep in mind that reductions are not an end in themselves. What made the start of reductions possible was the willingness of the democracies to maintain an adequate deterrent posture. What will sustain the process of reductions is the willingness to ensure that at every level of reductions, deterrence is maintained and preferably strengthened. Such a concept of "deterrent disarmament" must meet two strict criteria: first—to restate the basic concept—Western deterrence must be maintained with no less credibility or capacity than *before* each stage of reductions; and second, the capability for a conventional defense must not be weakened, and preferably should be strengthened, as a result of force reductions on both sides.

In order to apply these criteria, the new balance of forces must be carefully assessed before and during every stage of the arms control process. Such a concept of security, reconciling reductions, deterrence and defense for each foreseeable level of reductions, has yet to be defined. It is one of the most urgent tasks before our governments and must be geared to the political, economic and military circumstances likely to prevail in the 1990s. The political evolution of Europe, to be discussed later, must be a central feature of such a concept.

In developing a new concept of security, some of the following issues will have to be addressed:

- The terms of a strategic arms agreement must produce a more stable strategic relationship than would be the case in the absence of agreement. Any reduction of strategic arms must be accompanied by efforts to generate public and Congressional and parliamentary support for programs that might be required for survivability, such as mobile missiles or more submarines.

- Conventional arms control is now broadly accepted in the West. Yet current conventional imbalances and underlying geographic realities are highly favorable to the Soviet Union. These imbalances, moreover, have become far more critical in the wake of the removal of important nuclear forces under the INF agreement. It is essential for the democracies to determine what reduced level of conventional NATO forces is compatible with a conventional defense no less effective than at the present. All governments have an obligation to ensure that their defense efforts not fall below such a minimum level in the course of reductions—a difficult challenge in conditions where Soviet proposals will be at least partially designed to reduce Western forces beyond an acceptable military minimum.

- The relationship between further nuclear arms reductions and conventional arms control must be carefully evaluated. Gorbachev has singled out nuclear weapons and is pressing in effect for denuclearization—or at least for the denuclearization of Central Europe—an idea that appeals to some segments of Western public opinion. Yet it is in our view incompatible with deterrence. Moreover, another START agreement could be reached well before any conventional arms agreements can be completed. It is our view, however, that the final stages of its implementation should await completion of a conventional arms control agreement.

- The political impact of conventional force reductions in Europe—both Eastern and Western—will be profound. It must be related to the process of West European unification, the various ideas of a "Common European House" currently in vogue in Europe, and the role of the United States in such a design.

- A concept of "deterrent disarmament" must finally seek to resolve the debate over strategic defenses. Since President Reagan's original announcement of SDI, the focus of criticism has been on the broad goal of an invulnerable defense which, if at all achievable, is decades away. But there has been no thoughtful examination—in the United States or in the Alliance—of intermediate options, for example, to defend American ballistic missile sites, or Allied populations against small-scale attacks. It would be a fateful decision to forego defense altogether and leave populations open to any level of nuclear attacks.

In sum, the strategic and security relationship between East and West needs to be redefined. Arms control, whether regional or strategic, remains extremely important. But it must be related to the goals of larger security and foreign policy. It must be pursued in a manner that increases the opportunities for political accommodations, and in this regard, as discussed in the next sections, the role of Europe will become exceedingly important. Thus, we favor a policy of parallelism in which reductions are closely linked to a concept of a strong defense at every level and of the opportunities to make progress on political issues.

Regional Conflicts
Until recently, there has been an absence of a sense of urgency in resolving regional conflicts or in linking them closely with other aspects of East-West relations. Yet history shows that tensions arise more frequently as a result of political conflict than due to weapons deployments. Moreover, prolonged conflict or tensions in such areas— Korea, Indochina, the Middle East, and Central America—represent a human tragedy of immense proportions. The settlements in Afghanistan and Angola and the progress made in Cambodia are hopeful developments.

The inevitable transformations in the global balance are not likely to occur without crises. And U.S.-Soviet relations will be central to maintaining the peace. These looming transformations should receive systematic attention, for in the long run they will have even more far-reaching implications than arms control or trade.

One such challenge (discussed in the next section) concerns the emerging new relationship between Eastern and Western Europe. Conventional arms control negotiations will inevitably reopen the question of the political future of Eastern Europe, and so will the process of reform in the Soviet Union. So far, the Soviet Union has tied its military security to regimes in Eastern Europe whose instabilities create their own momentum. This represents a long-term danger even for the Soviet Union. We will deal in the section on East-West relations in Europe with our views on how to transform political relationships in Europe.

We cannot expect to eliminate all local conflicts, but our countries should seek to encourage peaceful change. At the same time, one of the important tests of a new East-West relationship is whether the Soviet Union is willing to forego the temptations of exploiting local conflicts.

The Future of Europe
It has long been recognized in the West, and by many in Eastern Europe too, that the relationship with Moscow imposed on these countries after World War II was artificial and, in the long run, unsustainable.

Communism could not satisfy the material needs of Eastern Europe,
still less its cultural and political aspirations. Post-World War II history
is replete with efforts by East European countries to change this
unnatural relationship by revolution or by more subtle means designed to avoid a Soviet counteraction.

Gorbachev's perestroika constitutes an admission that the Soviet
Communist economic system has not worked for the Soviet Union,
hence even less for Eastern Europe; glasnost implies that this fact can
and must be openly admitted. The economic inefficiency and challenge
to the legitimacy of the ruling Communist parties are more starkly
evident than ever. This underlying reality is the cause of growing
ferment.

Our countries face a dilemma in their policies toward Eastern
Europe. We are committed to see progress toward enabling the peoples
of Eastern Europe to determine their own future. But we do not wish
to provide a pretext for new Soviet intervention that would set back
the evolution toward liberty in Eastern Europe and strengthen more
conservative forces in the Soviet Union. Clearly, we should continue
to stress the differences between democracy in the West and the way
political systems actually function in the East. We should give support
to any movement toward market economies and democratic institutions. We should continue a strong effort to break down the barriers
to the freer flow of people and ideas across the center of Europe. And
we must insist on the removal of the so-called Brezhnev Doctrine
which has been used to justify Soviet military intervention in Eastern
Europe.

Mr. Gorbachev's phrase "a Common European House" ignores the
fundamental differences between Western Europe, Eastern Europe
and the Soviet Union. On one level, we can recognize in this phrase
the desire for a more open and peaceful pattern of relationships, a
framework provided for in the Helsinki Final Act and other CSCE
documents. In that sense, there is scope for collaboration in some
practical areas. Environmental problems, including nuclear safety,
and improvements in communications and transport are examples
deserving of high priority.

On another level, the concept of a "European House" can be inter-
preted as an effort to dissociate the United States from Europe. We
categorically reject any such policy.

Our European policy should, therefore, distinguish among three
separate European realities:

(1) Western Europe, composed of the 12 EC countries increasingly integrated into a single European Community with its own system of external relations, together with the EFTA countries.

(2) The Soviet Union, extending far into Asia and therefore not a fully European country.

(3) The countries of Central and Eastern Europe have a special character. They are members of the Warsaw Pact and as such participants in conventional arms control negotiations between East and West. At the same time, they have historically been part of Europe and they have a growing wish to participate in certain aspects at least of European unification, as well as to achieve greater control over their national political destinies.

For these countries, it is therefore important to *devise a category of association with the European Community based on Article 238 of the Treaty of Rome.*[†] This kind of association should be regarded as a new type of relationship adapted to the special circumstances of the countries concerned. This relationship will not include, for the foreseeable future, any political or security dimension. But such an agreement should be accompanied by a full commitment to implement all the obligations of the Helsinki accord and subsequent agreements regarding human rights together with effective provisions for monitoring them.

We suggest that the European Council (the Heads of State and Government of the European Community) should announce its intention to embark on an examination of the modalities of such an arrangement. This should not be linked specifically with the case of any single East European country, but should provide the framework for the kind of association which could ultimately be negotiated in detail with those countries which manifest their interest and meet the necessary conditions.

As to the relationship of Eastern Europe with the USSR, the key question is whether the USSR is prepared to undertake a reappraisal of its security interests in Eastern Europe. We note Gorbachev's statement that "security can no longer be assured by military means." We should seek new patterns in Eastern and Central Europe that would allow a political and economic evolution reflecting popular aspira-

---

[†]Article 238: "The Community may conclude with a third State, a union of States or an international organization agreements establishing an association involving reciprocal rights and obligations, common action and special procedures. These agreements shall be concluded by the Council, acting unanimously after consulting the Assembly. Where such agreements call for amendments to this Treaty, these amendments shall first be adopted in accordance with the procedure laid down in Article 236."

tions. Our countries should state clearly that they have no intention to challenge legitimate Soviet security interests. But we do not accept that these security interests include the right of military intervention in Eastern Europe or of imposing regimes rejected by the populations.

East-West Economic Relations
We have stated in an earlier section that we welcome perestroika to the degree that it brings the Soviet Union closer to market economics and to democratic institutions. Such an evolution would almost automatically make the Soviet Union an increasingly integral part of the world economy. Undoubtedly, this is what Gorbachev had in mind when he stated his intention that the Soviet Union should become a "normal" participant in international economic relations, with the ruble becoming convertible. We support this objective but wish to raise a number of questions with respect to it.

The first concerns the attitude of our countries toward normalized economic relations in such areas as trade, investments, non-military-related technological transfers, commercial loans and trade credits.

It is in the common interest of the Western countries to avoid periodic massive injections of credit into the Soviet Union: for the Soviet Union it would mean a situation of lasting indebtedness; for the industrialized democracies it would amount to open-ended support for an unbalanced economy—without the necessary fundamental reforms in prices, freer enterprises, and convertibility of the ruble—and a potentially irresponsible conduct of affairs. Thus, we advise against embarking on a global financing of the Soviet Union. But, in an environment of reduced international tensions, we do envisage supporting specific economic and social changes and reforms. If the Soviet Union reduces its military expenditures significantly and behaves responsibly in regional conflicts, we propose that our countries support activities that would promote economic change tending towards market economics and democratic institutions.

Specifically:

- The spread of Joint Ventures for the purpose of producing consumer goods should be encouraged. Western capital thus invested could be given the same degree of guarantee used for sales of capital goods. Such cover could be provided in part by a specialized institution to be created within the European Community or in the OECD.

- Financial support could be given to new institutions set up in the Soviet Union to provide finance or training for small businesses, new service industries and the private sector of agriculture.

- We favor that the Soviet Union be offered observer status in international institutions, such as GATT and the IMF. This may make it easier for the Soviet Union to adapt its own rules to normal international practice. For the same reasons, our countries ought to be ready to facilitate any decision by the USSR to bring the ruble closer to its market value, and to support initiatives toward convertibility. However, full membership by the Soviet Union in international economic institutions cannot be considered until it is clear that the Soviet Union is ready to accept the obligations of being a member, and that its economic system has been sufficiently altered to assure reciprocal benefits for its economic partners.

Sales of militarily sensitive goods or technology should be treated as an aspect of strategic rather than economic relationships. So long as the Soviet Union represents a potential threat, it is important to maintain controls on the sales of strategic items to the Soviet Union or its allies. To be effective, any such system must include all the key industrial democracies. This makes unavoidable mutual concessions and compromises within the framework of the basic principle.

To operate effectively, COCOM must enjoy the support of our governments and the understanding of our business communities. The rationale for the system and for restricting certain items must be convincing. In an era of improving East-West relations, closer consultation among our nations on strategic controls is essential both to ensure their solidarity and to develop an effective strategy for liberalizing these controls should a reduction of the threat to the West permit it.

The Role of the Soviet Union in Asia
There are basic differences between the geopolitical situation of Europe and that of Asia. There is a common cultural tradition in Europe which, with many variations, stretches from the Mediterranean through the Soviet Union. Asia is not only much more culturally diverse, but the Soviet Union is hardly a part of any Asian cultural tradition. There have been stable and coherent strategic alliances in Europe, with the Warsaw Pact on one side, NATO on the other. The European countries outside these pacts have confirmed policies of neutrality and are not a target of opportunity for either side. Asia is a region of bilateral alliances (even the Manila treaty is more bilateral than collective in character) and shifting alignments. There are many lines of actual or potential conflict outside of the main East-West framework, including mutual suspicions and conflicting relationships among the socialist countries of the region. The coherence of Europe is reflected in the Helsinki Accords, in which countries of both West and East reached

agreement on principles of relations and "confidence-building measures" in order to reduce tensions. Mr. Gorbachev has proposed a
Helsinki-type treaty for Asia, but in this more diverse environment,
the basis for confidence-building measures has yet to be laid. Unlike
Europe, many divisive post-World War II issues remain, including the
division of the Korean peninsula and the question of Japan's "Northern Territories."

Gorbachev's Soviet Union has made intense efforts to be accepted
as part of the Asia-Pacific region. Nevertheless, despite its enormous
Asian territories, the USSR is commonly viewed as an outsider.
Gorbachev's own emphasis on the theme of a "Common European
House" appears to Asians to reflect Moscow's orientation toward Europe rather than Asia. Most of the Soviet Pacific maritime areas are
closed to travel and trade. The Soviets most Asians come into contact
with are usually European. The Soviet Union looms large in Asia in
only one dimension—as a military power.

We urge that the reduction of the Soviet military presence in Europe
be accompanied by comparable reductions in Asia, including the maritime provinces facing Japan. We hope that the Soviet Union will work
constructively to defuse further tensions in the Korean peninsula, Indochina, and South Asia. We also urge a favorable resolution of the
territorial dispute between the Soviet Union and Japan involving
Soviet occupation of Japan's four northern islands. Our countries need
to strengthen their relationships with the People's Republic of China
and with India, which will be increasingly important regional actors.

Finally, there is the longer-term question of the relationship between the Soviet Union and the emerging Asia-Pacific community.
There should be no obstacle to the Soviet Union eventually becoming
a good partner in an Asia-Pacific community if Soviet military forces
in the region are reduced, pending issues are resolved one-by-one, and
the Soviet Union removes the barriers that now prevent its Asian
territories from truly cooperating with their neighbors.

The Protection of Human Rights
Our countries have a deep concern rooted in our basic values for the
personal freedom of all people including those of the Soviet Union and
Eastern European countries. We should promote the importance of
family ties across frontiers as well as exchanges, from professional
groups and scientists to athletes and artists. The Helsinki Accords
guarantee respect for basic human rights and the free flow of people,
ideas and information. The CSCE process has now developed criteria
to judge progress as well as a monitoring mechanism. In the Soviet

Union itself, Mr. Gorbachev has introduced some reforms and announced others. To be ultimately significant, these must be anchored in national legislation and binding international agreements and protected by adequate and independent judicial mechanisms. We insist that there is a link between moderation in foreign policy and democratic liberty at home.

Summary

An effective Western strategy must rest on two principles: our countries must work together and they must develop a positive agenda.

Gorbachev is a vigorous leader who has proven adept in seizing the initiative and in gaining the attention of the media. Western leaders should not find themselves on the defensive because of Gorbachev's flair for surprises and unconventional initiatives. This is all the more true because our democratic political systems and alliances require genuine consultations and consensus building.

Relations with the Soviet Union and its allies will remain a mixture of confrontation and cooperation, containment and dialogue. Thus, we need a positive and clear agenda that reflects our concept of the future of East-West relations and will also serve as a standard against which we can evaluate both Soviet initiatives and Soviet performance.

- The competitive relationship between East and West will not disappear, though it may diminish in importance relative to other trends in international relations. Four years of attempted reform in the USSR have opened new avenues for dialogue and cooperation, but they do not yet allow us to say that East-West relations are on a totally new footing. An overall reconciliation of conflicting interests is still a long-term, not an immediate objective. But we can build the basis of long-term reconciliation by solving some of the concrete problems covered in this report.

- Some of these issues have a regional character. From that point of view, the forthcoming NATO summit is of great importance in defining Western security and arms control policy. There are, in addition, underlying issues of a global character which should engage the Pacific allies as well as the nations bordering the Atlantic. The 1983 Williamsburg economic summit of the industrial democracies provides an example of effective consultation and common action by the industrial democracies. The forthcoming economic summit in Paris provides another important opportunity for a full airing of views on East-West relations, including common security interests, among the leaders of the major industrial democracies.

- Changes in the Soviet domestic order are primarily the concern of the Soviet people, but positive reforms should be encouraged, as long as they move the Soviet Union closer to Western practices of market economics and democratic institutions. Such changes, however, cannot be the principal objective of Western policy, which must be based on Soviet performance in international relations.

- Our countries must continue to manage the East-West relationship with no less firmness and prudence than in the past, but in a way that takes full account of the changes in both atmosphere and substance. In other words, we should be prepared to cooperate with the Soviet Union selectively in the context of the Soviet Union's adopting a more conciliatory foreign policy as well as more liberalized and democratic measures, but not unconditionally.

To formulate a common strategy toward the Soviet Union requires criteria by which the West can test its effectiveness and gauge the pace of progress. Important checkpoints would be:

(1) Progress in the East-West security dialogue, both military and political:

- The arms control process should be related more systematically to a concept of negotiations covering the political as well as the military aspects of security.

- Both East and West seem prepared to engage in the progressive reductions of military expenditures and forces. At every level, these reductions must meet the test of continued effectiveness of the Western capability to prevent aggression and discourage military adventures.

- Therefore, while the United States and the NATO member states should vigorously press the Soviet Union to reduce its conventional forces deployed in the European theater, beyond the unilateral cuts already announced, the objective should be to reach a point where there would be a minimal danger of a surprise attack, and little potential for a massive and rapid build-up from reserves in European Russia.

- The West must carefully examine the linkage between further nuclear arms control and conventional arms reductions, especially in Europe. The two ought to proceed in some general relationship.

- Soviet redeployment in Europe, however, cannot be shifted to Asia; and the process of force reductions by the Soviet Union should apply to Asia as well as to Europe. We urge a favorable resolution of the territorial dispute between the Soviet Union and Japan involving Soviet occupation of Japan's four northern islands.

(2) Events in Afghanistan, Angola and Cambodia are encouraging signs of a new appreciation of the limits of Soviet capabilities; but Moscow will need to demonstrate that this is more than tactical expediency. What is needed is the renunciation, by Moscow, in principle, and as a matter of consistent practice, of any exploitation of regional crises.

(3) The political future of the countries of Eastern Europe now part of the Warsaw Pact must receive special attention. Their relationship to legitimate Soviet security interests will be dealt with in the ongoing arms control negotiations. On the other hand, Europe would return to a more natural relationship when these nations articulate their own relationship to Western Europe and their own internal political structure. The nations of Eastern and Central Europe now part of the Warsaw Pact should be free to undertake an economic association with the European Community based on Article 238 of the Treaty of Rome. And the Soviet Union should apply to Eastern Europe the principles of non-intervention in domestic affairs put forward by Gorbachev before the UN General Assembly.

(4) The United States, Canada and West European nations have both the right and obligation to require the Soviet Union to abide by the Helsinki Final Act and subsequent accords in the CSCE process, including the last agreements reached in Vienna. Some of the new attitudes in Moscow should help to create the conditions for further advances in the areas to which the West has always attached special importance, such as human rights and the free flow of people, ideas and information. The more these advances can be anchored in binding agreements and national legislation, the greater can be our trust in their permanence.

(5) There needs to be a common attitude toward East-West economic relations:

- Unstructured and uncoordinated concessions must be avoided.

- East-West economic relations must reflect mutual interests. Obviously, the USSR does not qualify for the kind of concessionary terms that are appropriate in the Third World. Western credits and transfer of technology are no substitutes for adequate economic policies, rational reforms and a national effort.

- We welcome those economic reforms in the USSR that are oriented toward creating a market-related economic structure. But we warn against "political trade" that would depart from the normal rules and practices for developing international trade. While creating a climate of confidence for Western businessmen, the industrial democracies must be careful lest the largely uncoordinated Western credit system should help to create another debt crisis in Eastern Europe and the Soviet Union.

- We do not favor financing the Soviet Union as a political entity. We do propose to support, and perhaps to finance, those changes in the Soviet Union's economic structure that will make it more compatible with Western practices and values—provided the Soviet Union carries out a major reduction of its military expenditures and conducts a conciliatory foreign policy. The modernization of those aspects of the Soviet economy that promote competition and a climate of pluralism, e.g., Joint Ventures, managerial training and technical assistance to encourage individual private farming, deserve attention.

- Our countries should welcome Soviet and Eastern European participation in international economic insitutions when these countries are ready to assume the obligations of such institutions and can meet the normal tests for entry. In the meantime, we support their admission to observer status.

- Our countries should be open to supporting moves by the Soviet Union to adjust the value of the ruble or to take the initiative in creating the conditions for the partial or full convertibility of the ruble.

- There were good reasons for establishing COCOM, and there are good reasons for maintaining it. The system must operate effectively and fairly to inspire confidence among the very businessmen that, in the nature of the system, it must inevitably penalize.

(6) The way is open for a new approach to relations in the Third World. Both sides should refrain from exacerbating conflicts and seek by joint efforts to resolve them. In addition, we would expect the Soviet Union to strengthen its contributions to the economic development of the Third World by participating in relevant international economic institutions.

Concluding Remarks

The opportunity to put East-West relations on a new foundation is before our countries. To seize this opportunity, our countries must act on the basis of careful analysis, not wishful thinking. We need to recognize that qualitative changes are occurring in the Soviet Union, but be realistic about the limits and uncertainties of change. Our countries should enhance their consultations on the developments occurring in the Soviet Union and their implications, and our countries should increase their efforts to develop a common strategy for the West. We should make it clear to our publics that on this basis we are prepared to make every effort and explore every possibility toward achieving a constructive East-West partnership in the search for peace.

The Trilateral Process

This report is the joint responsibility of the three principals.

Although only the principals are responsible for the analysis and conclusions, each has been assisted by an associate author. Working with Henry Kissinger has been William Hyland, Editor of *Foreign Affairs* and former U.S. Deputy Assistant to the President for National Security Affairs. Working with Valéry Giscard d'Estaing has been Sir Julian Bullard, who in 1988 stepped down as British Ambassador to the Federal Republic of Germany and retired from the diplomatic service. Sir Julian discussed ideas for the report with European members of the Trilateral Commission assembled for their regional meeting in Oslo at the beginning of October 1988. He also consulted with officials and Trilateral members during visits to Madrid, Lisbon, Brussels, The Hague, Copenhagen, Rome, Bonn and London. The associate author working with Yasuhiro Nakasone was Professor Hiroshi Kimura of the Slavic Research Center at Hokkaido University. Several other persons also assisted Mr. Nakasone as members of a study group which met a number of times in the course of the project. Valuable drafting assistance was provided by Charles E. Morrison, Senior Research Associate at the Japan Center for International Exchange in Tokyo and Special Assistant to the President of the East-West Center in Hawaii.

The principals and associates—along with Georges Berthoin, David Rockefeller and Yoshio Okawara from the leadership of the Trilateral Commission—held discussions with Mikhail Gorbachev and other Soviet leaders in Moscow on January 16-18, 1989. The Trilateral side is very grateful to the Presidium of the Supreme Soviet of the U.S.S.R. for so ably serving as host for our delegation.

The work on this project began with a series of bilateral meetings among the principals in the spring and summer of 1988. The principals and associates met together in London on September 20-21, 1988, to discuss the thrust of the report and the upcoming trip to Moscow. Further bilateral discussions ensued before the principals and associates gathered again, in Paris on January 15, 1989, just before departure for Moscow. Several additional meetings among the principals took place in March 1989. An authors' meeting in Paris on April 8 preceded discussion of the report in the annual meeting of the Trilateral Commission on April 10. The report was finalized shortly thereafter.